7587 2944

The Great ShaRk ReScue

Saving the Whale Sharks

Sandra Markle

Millbrook Press • Minneapolis

For Rhonda Jenkins and the children at Kendall Elementary School in Naperville, Illinois

 The graphics that appear throughout the book represent zooplankton, the tiny ocean animals and fish eggs that are the main part of a whale shark's diet.

Acknowledgments: The author would like to thank the following people for sharing their enthusiasm and expertise: Dr. William B. Driggers III, research fishery biologist, National Marine Fisheries Service; Dr. Neil Hammerschlag, director, Shark Research & Conservation Program, University of Miami; Dr. Eric Hoffmayer, fishery biologist, National Oceanic and Atmospheric Administration, National Marine Fisheries Service; Dr. Robert Hueter, director, Shark Research Center at the Mote Marine Laboratory in Florida; Dr. Chris Lowe, director, Shark Lab at California State University–Long Beach; Rafael de la Parra, executive director, Ch'ooj Ajauil AC, Cancun; Dr. Simon J. Pierce, principal scientist at the Marine Megafauna Foundation, California; Dr. Jennifer Schmidt, director of science and research, Shark Research Institute, Princeton, New Jersey; and Dr. James Sulikowski, director, Sulikowski Shark and Fish Research Lab, University of New England.

A special thank-you to Skip Jeffery for his loving support during the creative process.

Millbrook Press™
An imprint of Lerner Publishing Group, Inc.
241 First Avenue North
Minneapolis, MN 55401 USA

For reading levels and more information, look up this title at www.lernerbooks.com.

Main body text set in Metro Office.
Typeface provided by Linotype AG.

Library of Congress Cataloging-in-Publication Data

Names: Markle, Sandra, author.
Title: The great shark rescue : saving the whale sharks / by Sandra Markle.
Description: Minneapolis : Millbrook Press, [2019] | Series: Sandra Markle's science discoveries | Includes bibliographical references and index.
Identifiers: LCCN 2018038332 (print) | LCCN 2018039696 (ebook) | ISBN 9781541562646 (eb pdf) | ISBN 9781541510418 (lb : alk. paper)
Subjects: LCSH: Whale shark—Juvenile literature. | Endangered species—Conservation—Juvenile literature.
Classification: LCC QL638.95.R4 (ebook) | LCC QL638.95.R4 M37 2019 (print) | DDC 597.3/3—dc23

LC record available at https://lccn.loc.gov/2018038332

Manufactured in the United States of America
1-43963-33971-3/7/2019

TABLE OF CONTENTS

Trapped ! — 4

Whale Sharks in Trouble — 8

Oceans of Problems — 13

Ocean Detective Tools — 22

A Mysterious Life — 30

Rescued! — 36

Great White Sharks Need Help Too — 40

Author's Note – 42

Did You Know? – 43

Timeline – 44

Source Notes – 45

Glossary – 46

Find Out More – 47

Index – 48

TRAPPED !

With its huge mouth open, a whale shark swims slowly near the surface close to Mafia Island off the coast of Tanzania. The 16-foot-long (4.8 m) giant is feeding on lots of tiny, shrimplike krill and a few little fish. Next, a 22-foot-long (6.7 m) whale shark arrives to share this feast.

As big as these giants are, they're both juveniles and still have some growing to do. Whale sharks are the largest fish in the ocean. Adults can grow to be as much as 40 feet (12 m) long—as long as the average school bus. Of course, eating as much as they can is just what these young ones need to grow even bigger and become mature adults. So they keep on swimming and feeding.

Sharks are a kind of fish, and whale sharks are the largest fish in the ocean.

Some fishing ships use purse seine nets that stretch almost a mile (1.6 km) to catch large numbers of fish.

All at once, a big net blocks their way. The whale sharks dive and turn, trying to swim under or around the net. But it's everywhere. The young whale sharks have been caught in a purse seine, a type of fishing net used by a fishing boat. As the boat sails in a circle, floats keep the upper edge of the net at the surface. A chain of weights on a cable runs along the lower edge of the net to sink it deep into the water. Then the fishing crew slowly hauls the cable onto the boat, pulling the sides of the net together and capturing fish inside the net bag. This time, the catch includes the two juvenile whale sharks.

The crew didn't plan to catch the whale sharks, but they're trapped anyway. And as the smaller whale shark struggles to be free, it becomes entangled in the net.

What will happen to the trapped whale sharks?

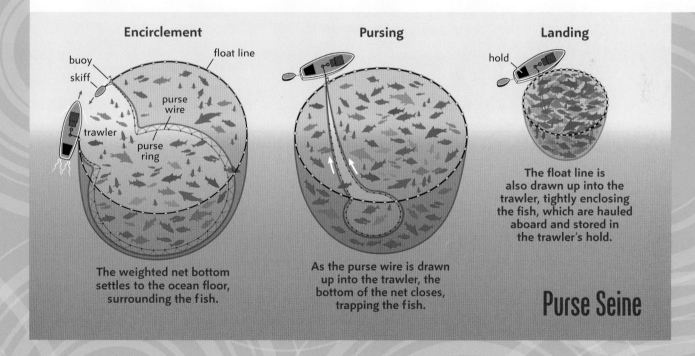

Encirclement

buoy
float line
skiff
purse wire
trawler
purse ring

The weighted net bottom settles to the ocean floor, surrounding the fish.

Pursing

As the purse wire is drawn up into the trawler, the bottom of the net closes, trapping the fish.

Landing

hold

The float line is also drawn up into the trawler, tightly enclosing the fish, which are hauled aboard and stored in the trawler's hold.

Purse Seine

WHALE SHARKS IN TROUBLE

The whale shark population can't afford to lose these two young, healthy sharks. In recent years, the number of whale sharks seriously decreased around the world. Whale shark experts estimate, based on sightings, that the population has shrunk to half of what it was seventy-five years ago. By the end of 2018, researchers identified only 9,756 whale sharks.*

*You can check the Wildbook for Whale Sharks at https://www.whaleshark.org to find the most recent number of whale sharks.

Researchers believe whale sharks don't become mature adults until they're between twenty and thirty years old and over 26 feet (8 m) long.

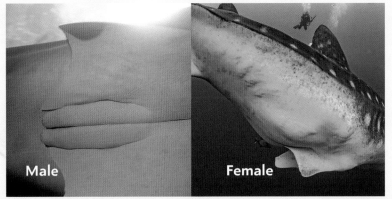

Male

Female

Divers swimming under a whale shark can identify a male because it has claspers, modified parts of two pelvic fins. When divers don't see the claspers, they know the whale shark is female.

Scientists are concerned for the future of the whale shark population because most of the sharks they're seeing are smaller juvenile males, younger males that aren't yet ready to reproduce. Whale shark expert James Sulikowski said, "Researchers can't put a number on how many mature adults would make a healthy population. But we know, globally, whale sharks are considered endangered because their populations are generally decreasing."

In 2016, because fewer whale sharks were observed—and most of those were juvenile males—the International Union for Conservation of Nature (IUCN) changed the whale shark's status. It went from Vulnerable (likely to become endangered unless the threats to their survival diminish) to Endangered (at risk of becoming extinct). If they became extinct, no more would exist.

What is threatening the survival of whale sharks?

A Whale Shark Is a Shark

Whale sharks are ocean giants like whales. However, a whale shark is not a whale. It's the largest kind of shark. Check out some ways whale sharks are different from whales—and a few ways they're different from other kinds of sharks.

Humpback Whale

HUMPBACK WHALE

- Has lungs and must surface to breathe through the blowhole on top of its head
- Is warm-blooded (energy from food produces body heat to regulate body temperature)
- Has a horizontal tail that it moves up and down to propel itself through the water
- Has its mouth at the end of its nose
- Has a skeleton of bones and body covered with smooth skin
- Mother produces milk for young (that can nurse up to two years, depending on size)

Whale Shark

WHALE SHARK

- Has gills for breathing underwater (five gill slits on each side of its body)
- Is cold-blooded (unable to regulate body temperature, so it's always similar to the water temperature around it)
- Has a vertical tail like a shark, but it uses its whole body to propel itself through the water, unlike other sharks that just move their tail and rear
- Has its mouth at the end of its nose (unlike some sharks, which have it under a snout)
- Has a skeleton of cartilage (the rubbery material inside human ears) and body covered with denticles (toothlike scales)
- Probably does not care for its young (assumed by researchers because other sharks don't care for their young, but too little is known about whale shark young to be completely sure)

OCEANS OF PROBLEMS

A key threat to adult whale sharks is commercial fishing. It's unfortunate when fishing boats accidentally catch whale sharks, like the trapped young males. But it's tragic when whale sharks are caught on purpose.

A single juvenile-sized whale shark is worth about $30,000 for all of its parts. A bigger adult is worth even more. Some fishing crews are willing to risk fines if caught with a dead whale shark because of a whale shark's high value. Restaurants in Asia use whale shark fins to make shark fin soup—considered a special delicacy and usually very expensive. Some people display whale shark fins because of their great size. Manufacturers of leather items buy the leathery skin. And companies that make fish oil supplements buy the oil from whale shark body fat.

It isn't always possible to know when whale sharks are killed illegally. Pakistani fishermen claimed this 40-foot-long (12 m) whale shark was found floating dead.

Climate change is also affecting whale sharks. Since the late nineteenth century, Earth's average air and water temperatures have been warming. This climate change has been changing wind patterns as well as ocean temperatures. Whale shark gathering sites—locations teeming with massive concentrations of food—have changed as a result. Those gathering sites usually start with an upwelling: offshore winds push on the surface water and create a rising current. Then the rising current carries nutrients up to the warm surface water. The nutrients allow phytoplankton (tiny ocean plant life) to grow and bloom. Zooplankton (tiny ocean animal life) gather to feed on the phytoplankton. Fish, such as little tunny, gather to feed on zooplankton. The fish also reproduce, releasing lots of eggs into the water. Little tunny eggs and other fish eggs are high-energy whale shark food. The whale sharks arrive to feast at the top of this food chain.

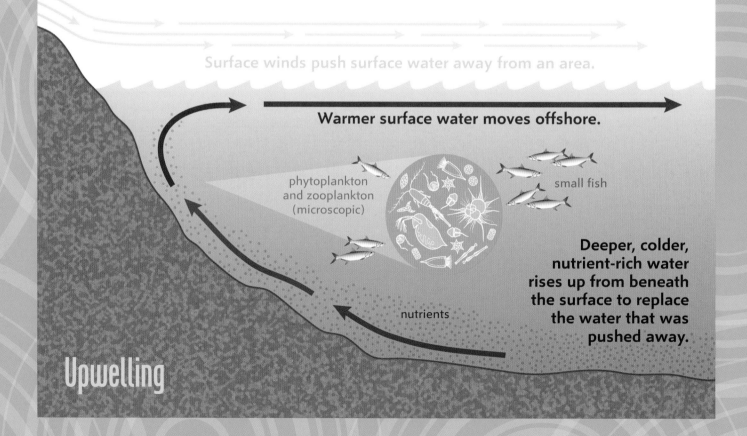

Surface winds push surface water away from an area.

Warmer surface water moves offshore.

phytoplankton and zooplankton (microscopic)

small fish

Deeper, colder, nutrient-rich water rises up from beneath the surface to replace the water that was pushed away.

nutrients

Upwelling

This whale shark is feeding on lots of little anchovies and even smaller zooplankton.

Like any animal at the top of a food chain, whale sharks are key members of their ocean ecosystem. They have a huge effect in their gathering sites. If there were fewer—or no—whale sharks, how would the populations of plankton and small fish change? Scientists are looking into this, but they don't yet know the answer. For example, what would happen if all of those millions of fish eggs the whale sharks eat hatched and the young fish grew up to compete for food?

Where whale sharks gather to feed isn't the only thing that's changed. Whale sharks live according to what scientists call the Goldilocks factor. These giants need the water they swim through to be just the right temperature, neither too cold nor too warm. That's because they don't have much insulating body fat. They have thick skin, up to 6 to 8 inches (15 to 20 cm) thick. But that isn't enough to protect their body from overheating or from losing vital body heat when they dive into the cold ocean depths. So climate change that affects ocean temperatures is also altering the migration routes whale sharks take to reach their gathering sites.

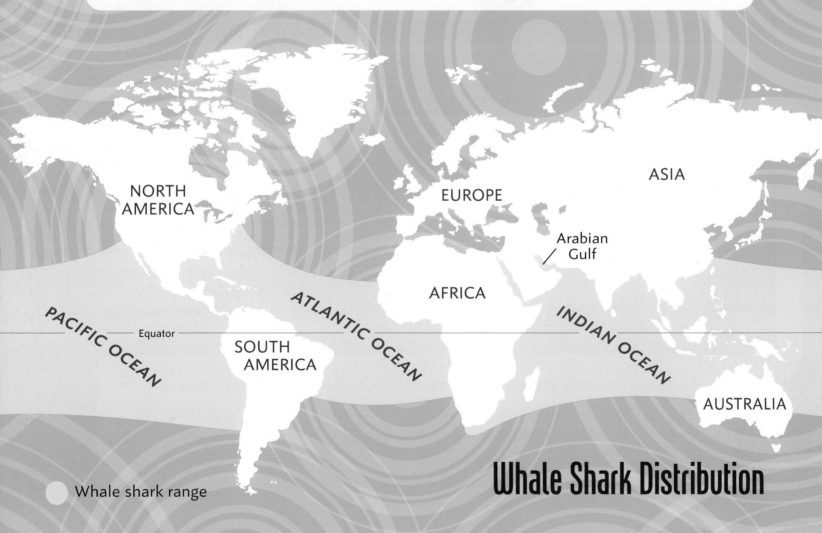

Whale Shark Distribution

Whale shark range

Whale sharks need the water temperature to be between 78.8°F and 86°F (26°C and 30°C). In the Arabian Gulf, whale sharks feed in surface water that may reach 95°F (35°C), but researchers believe the whale sharks regularly dive deeper into cooler water to cool off.

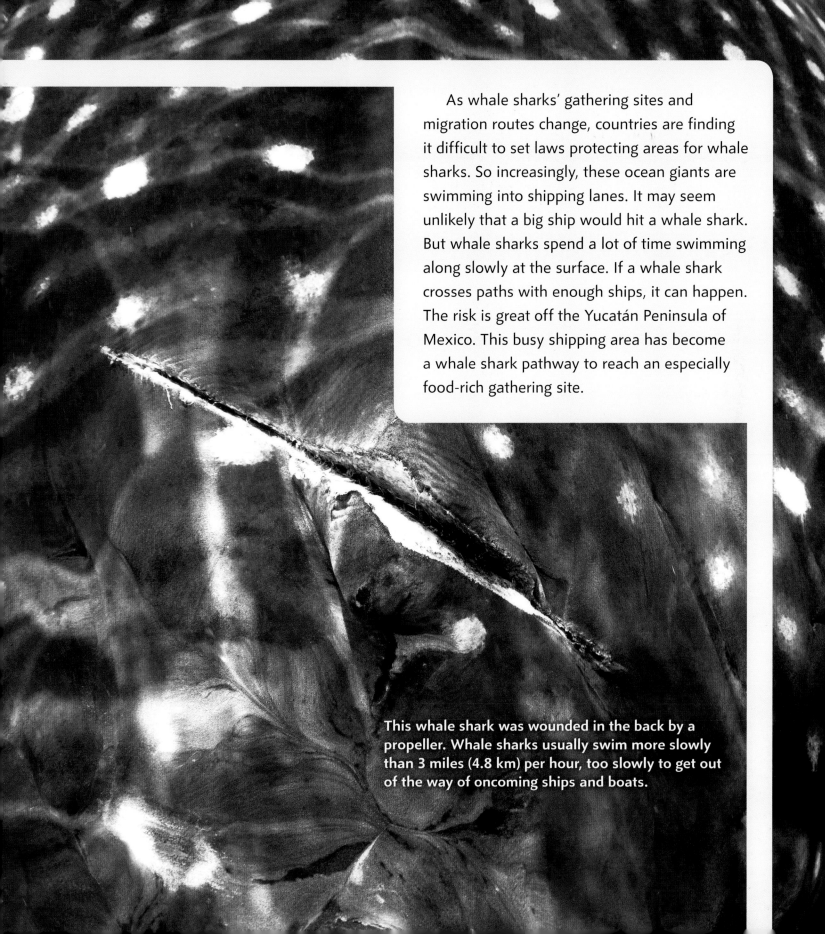

As whale sharks' gathering sites and migration routes change, countries are finding it difficult to set laws protecting areas for whale sharks. So increasingly, these ocean giants are swimming into shipping lanes. It may seem unlikely that a big ship would hit a whale shark. But whale sharks spend a lot of time swimming along slowly at the surface. If a whale shark crosses paths with enough ships, it can happen. The risk is great off the Yucatán Peninsula of Mexico. This busy shipping area has become a whale shark pathway to reach an especially food-rich gathering site.

This whale shark was wounded in the back by a propeller. Whale sharks usually swim more slowly than 3 miles (4.8 km) per hour, too slowly to get out of the way of oncoming ships and boats.

Dinnertime

Whale sharks are filter feeders. So to eat, a whale shark opens its wide mouth and swims straight ahead or straight up from the depths. This pushes water carrying plankton and small fish into its mouth and out through its gills, the body parts that take oxygen from the water and expel carbon dioxide. Whale sharks' mouths are about 4 feet (1.2 m) wide. A whale shark can also swim along below the surface, opening and closing its mouth, to suck in water.

As the water enters the whale shark's mouth on its way to the gills, it passes through twenty sievelike filter pads (ten on each side). The pads are set at an angle to the water flow so bigger bits in the water, such as the zooplankton and small fish, bounce off toward the back of the whale shark's mouth. These bits pile up.

A whale shark has 300 to 350 rows of tiny, backward-pointing teeth lined up just inside its mouth along its upper and lower jaws. That's about 3,000 teeth. Researchers aren't sure what these do, but they believe the teeth help keep tiny prey trapped inside the whale shark's mouth.

Every once in a while, the whale shark takes a big swallow by shutting its mouth and blasting the water out through its gills rather than letting it flow out. That swallow pushes the food down the whale shark's throat—a tube no bigger around than a softball.

Researcher Simon Pierce said, "When food is plentiful, we've observed whale sharks feeding for about eight hours a day. And we roughly estimate each eats as much as 314 pounds (142 kg) of phytoplankton in a day."

Experts estimate a feeding whale shark can filter enough water to fill an Olympic-sized swimming pool about every four hours.

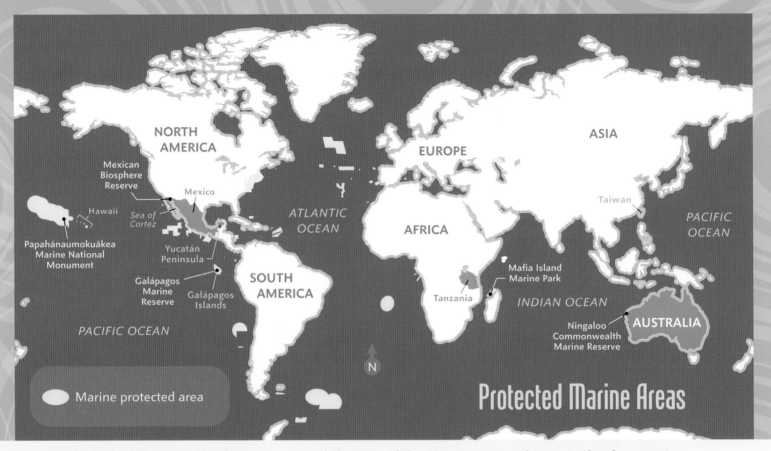

NORTH
AMERICA

Mexican
Biosphere
Reserve

Mexico

Hawaii   Sea of
              Cortez

Papahānaumokuākea
Marine National
Monument

Yucatán
Peninsula

Galápagos
Marine   Galápagos
Reserve   Islands

EUROPE

ASIA

Taiwan

ATLANTIC
OCEAN

AFRICA

PACIFIC
OCEAN

SOUTH
AMERICA

Mafia Island
Marine Park

Tanzania   INDIAN OCEAN

PACIFIC OCEAN

N

Ningaloo
Commonwealth
Marine Reserve

AUSTRALIA

Marine protected area

Protected Marine Areas

In 2016 President Barack Obama increased the size of the Hawaiian Papahānaumokuākea Marine National Monument, established in 2006 by President George W. Bush. It covers 582,578 square miles (1.5 million sq. km), an area larger than all the US land-based national parks combined.

Countries created ocean reserves to protect those locations where whale sharks gather each year. The Mexican Biosphere Reserve is near the whale shark gathering site off the Yucatán Peninsula, the Galápagos Marine Reserve is near the Galápagos Islands gathering site, and the Ningaloo Commonwealth Marine Reserve is near the gathering site by Ningaloo Reef off Australia. Within reserves, fishing is limited, oil exploration is controlled, and ecotourism—opportunities to swim with whale sharks and observe other endangered animals—is regulated. But as climate change alters the location of upwellings, whale shark gathering sites move too. Since 2009 researchers have increasingly observed whale sharks gathering outside the Mexican Biosphere Reserve in an area called the *afuera* (the outside).

Rafael de la Parra, who is working to protect whale sharks in the area, said, "Lots of whale sharks are now gathering in the *afuera*, mainly in July and August." So researchers are urging the Mexican government to add the *afuera* to the protected ocean reserve. And they're working to learn more about the lives and behavior of whale sharks so they can protect them the rest of the year when they're away from those gathering sites.

But how can researchers study whale sharks as they swim through Earth's vast oceans?

In 2016, during just one pass of the Mexican Biosphere Reserve in a plane, researchers counted five hundred whale sharks. In 2017 there were fewer but still hundreds.

OCEAN DETECTIVE TOOLS

Fortunately, thanks to new technologies, researchers have better ways to investigate whale sharks. One device for collecting information about whale shark behavior is the satellite archival tag (SAT). *Archival* means that the tag stores data until it's able to transmit it. It can only transmit when the whale shark swims near enough to the ocean's surface that the tag on its dorsal fin (on top of the back) is above water. A radio signal sends the data to satellites circling Earth. The tag can operate for up to two years, the life of the battery. The data it sends includes the whale shark's dive depths and the exact location where it surfaced.

A diver with a pole spear shoots a tag into the base of the whale shark's dorsal fin.

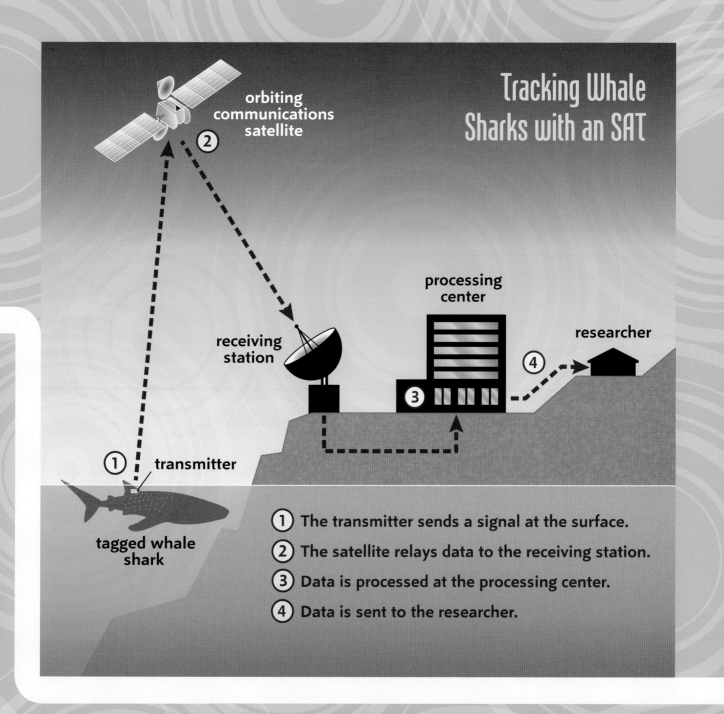

Tracking Whale Sharks with an SAT

orbiting communications satellite

② ①

receiving station

processing center

researcher

④

③

① transmitter

tagged whale shark

① The transmitter sends a signal at the surface.

② The satellite relays data to the receiving station.

③ Data is processed at the processing center.

④ Data is sent to the researcher.

A satellite receives data from a transmitter on the ocean's surface. It then sends the data to a processing center, and from there the data goes to researchers.

To investigate whale shark life underwater, researchers use another kind of satellite tag, a pop-up satellite archival tag (PSAT). Like the SAT, this tag provides data on the whale shark's geographic locations. At regular intervals, the PSAT also records depth and water temperature, collecting information about the whale shark's environment.

Unlike an SAT, the PSAT is set to stay attached to a whale shark for a set amount of time, usually six months. Then it releases, floats to the surface, and transmits its data. Simon Pierce explained, "We know the pups [infants] are doing something different from the juveniles. Plus it seems males and females are doing something different from each other. So, if we're going to help the whole population, the challenge is to figure out what each group is actually doing." With the help of the PSAT, scientists are hoping to learn more about the behavior of juvenile whale sharks versus adults, such as the depths they travel at or their water temperature preferences.

Researchers have discovered some whale sharks are residents of one ocean area, spending most of their time there. Others migrate between two areas. And still others are wanderers, traveling as far as 1,000 miles (1,609 km) in just a few weeks.

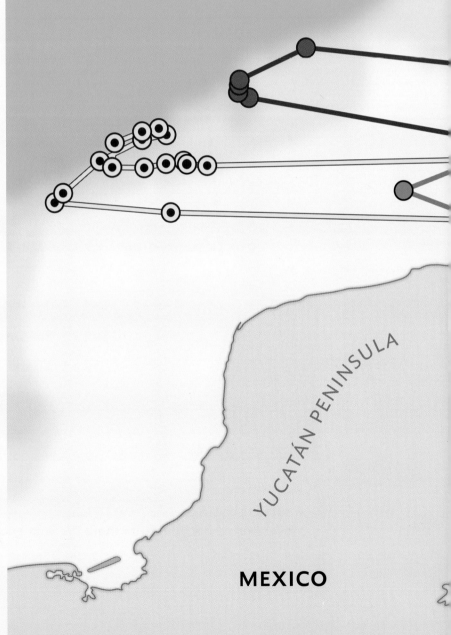

The trails of colored dots track the travels researchers recorded for individual tagged whale sharks.

YUCATÁN PENINSULA

MEXICO

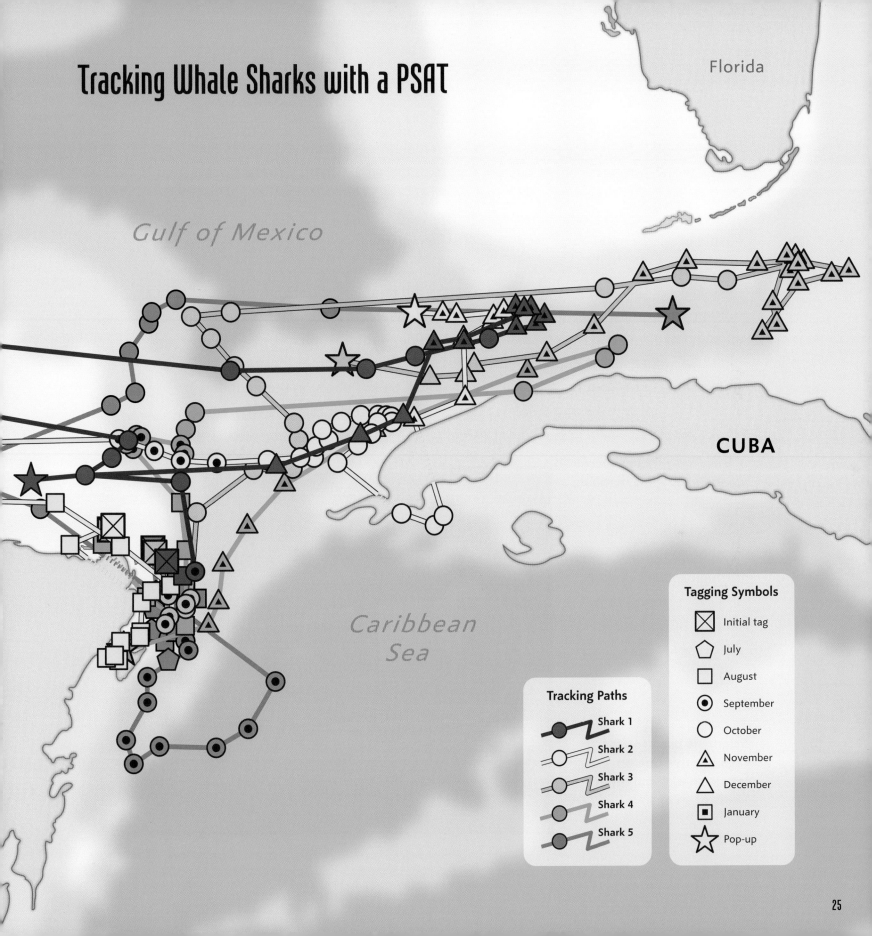

Tracking Whale Sharks with a PSAT

Florida

Gulf of Mexico

CUBA

Caribbean
Sea

Tracking Paths

- ━━●━ Shark 1
- ──○─ Shark 2
- ──○─ Shark 3
- ──●─ Shark 4
- ──●─ Shark 5

Tagging Symbols

- ⊠ Initial tag
- ⬠ July
- ☐ August
- ⊙ September
- ○ October
- △ November
- △ December
- ▪ January
- ☆ Pop-up

Another tool, the Wave Glider SV3, a drone (a remote-controlled, pilotless device), lets researchers track whale shark behavior in real time and from a distance. First, researchers attach an acoustic tag to the base of the whale shark's dorsal fin. Every sixty seconds, the tag emits a ping, an underwater sound signal. Each whale shark's acoustic tag is set to emit a different ping. These acoustic tags let the Wave Glider SV3 track and collect data about individual whale sharks that are close enough for it to detect the pings.

The Wave Glider SV3 drone has two parts—the float and the slightly smaller subunit—connected by a 26-foot (8 m) cord. Underwater, the subunit's wings move up and down with the waves, creating a swimming motion. That propels the Wave Glider SV3 along at a speed of about 3 miles (4.8 km) per hour. At the surface, the 10-foot-long (3 m) float is packed with equipment. Solar panels on the float power all the onboard sensors and systems. An onboard computer programs whether the Wave Glider SV3 floats in one place, "listening" for whale sharks in the area, or patrols a grid searching for acoustic pings. Whenever it detects a ping, it transmits the ID and location to researchers through cellular systems (if it's near shore) or by satellite (if it's far out in the ocean).

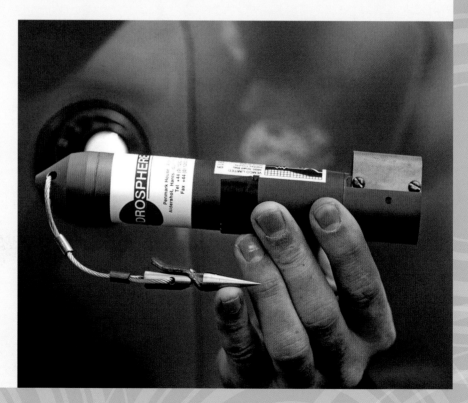

Scientists use acoustic tags like this one on whale sharks and other kinds of sharks.

The float also carries a variety of other sensors, depending on what information the researchers want to record. These include water temperature and the presence of chlorophyll—a green pigment that aids in the growth of phytoplankton, food for the zooplankton that whale sharks feed on.

Thanks to the Wave Glider SV3, researchers are gaining new insights into whale shark migration. They're also expanding their knowledge of the ocean conditions that are part of the Goldilocks factor—water that's neither too warm nor too cold—for whale sharks.

The Wave Glider SV3 operates on its own for about a year.

The Crittercam lets researchers watch whale shark behavior underwater in its natural environment. This watertight device is full of instruments attached to a big collar. A diver loops the collar over a whale shark's dorsal fin and clamps it in place. Then the Crittercam's camera records whatever is straight ahead. After about six hours, the onboard computer system triggers the clamp to release the collar. The Crittercam floats to the surface, and there it emits a radio beacon that lets researchers find and recover it.

The Crittercam is providing researchers with some never-before-possible information about whale sharks, such as how they find an area rich with food.

National Geographic marine biologist Greg Marshall invented the Crittercam in 1986. He got the idea from watching a remora (suckerfish) hitch a ride on a shark.

Spot On!

Researchers found they can identify and study individual whale sharks because each has a one-of-a-kind pattern of spots and stripes. A whale shark's pattern is as unique as a human fingerprint. Unlike some other sharks, such as zebra sharks that have skin coloration changes as they mature, a whale shark has the same telltale pattern its whole life.

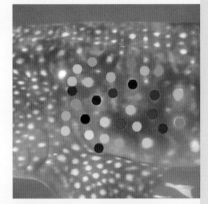

To make sure there's no confusion when experts record each whale shark's identifying pattern, it's always checked in exactly the same way. Researchers focus on the whale shark's spots as they appear on the left side behind the gill slits and above the pectoral (side) fin. Researchers take a picture of this area and enter it—along with an identifying number—into the Wildbook for Whale Sharks. Simon Pierce and other researchers started collecting results in this database in 2003 and reporting them online in 2004. Each time researchers photograph a whale shark, a dot is placed on each spot in its pattern. Next, a computer checks the dot pattern against the whale shark database. New whale sharks are entered into the database. Researchers log any previously identified whale shark's geographic location to track its travels.

Since 1994 Australian researcher Brad Norman has watched and studied two male whale sharks, nicknamed Zorro and Stumpy, thanks to their identifying spots.

The slits are the whale shark's gills. Scientists use the spot pattern directly behind the gills and above the pectoral fin on the left side for identification.

Scientists only very rarely find whale shark pups like this one to study. Though it's smaller, its body shape and appearance are similar to the adult on page 11. Check it out.

A MYSTERIOUS LIFE

What will it take to help whale sharks survive? Because so little is known about their lives, no one knows exactly how to help them.

In 1995 researchers learned something important about a whale shark's life cycle. A commercial fishing ship caught a pregnant female whale shark off the coast of Taiwan. Whale shark fishing was legal at that time. As the crew began to cut up their giant catch, they realized this whale shark was unusual— she was pregnant. So they reported their catch to the National Taiwan Ocean University. Excited at the news, researchers rushed to examine this rare whale shark.

Inside the pregnant female, researchers discovered over three hundred pups. Some were still inside their egg cases. Some had hatched and were in the uterus, ready to be born. Because of that, researchers learned whale shark pups develop inside eggs but are kept inside their mother's body until they grow enough to stay safe and find food on their own. And because the pups were at different stages of development, scientists believe the females probably give birth to some of the pups at one time. The others continue to develop until they're large enough and strong enough to live on their own.

The pups in the pregnant female were just 16 to 24 inches (40 to 60 cm) long. So researchers also wondered how such small pups could escape becoming dinner for bigger predators. Twelve years later, they discovered a clue to help them solve that mystery too.

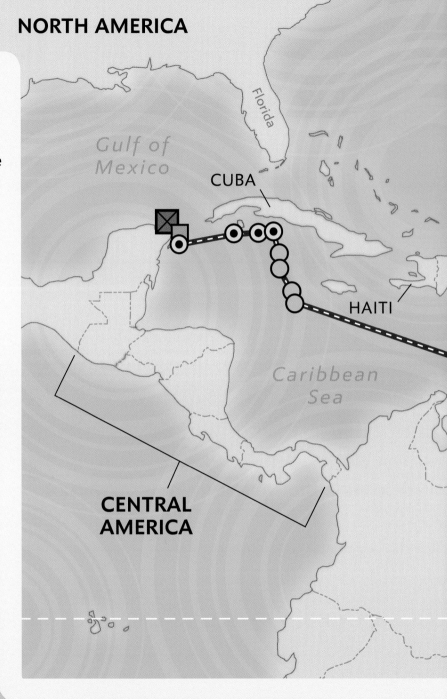

NORTH AMERICA

In 2007 Robert Hueter was studying whale sharks at a gathering site in the Atlantic Ocean off the Yucatán Peninsula of Mexico. He discovered an adult female whale shark with a very swollen belly and guessed that she was pregnant. So Hueter's team attached a PSAT to her dorsal fin. Then they tracked the female as she left the gathering site and swam through the Atlantic Ocean. He hoped to learn where the whale shark they nicknamed Rio Lady released her pups.

Gulf of Mexico

CUBA

Florida

HAITI

Caribbean Sea

CENTRAL AMERICA

Check where Rio Lady went during the different months of her journey.

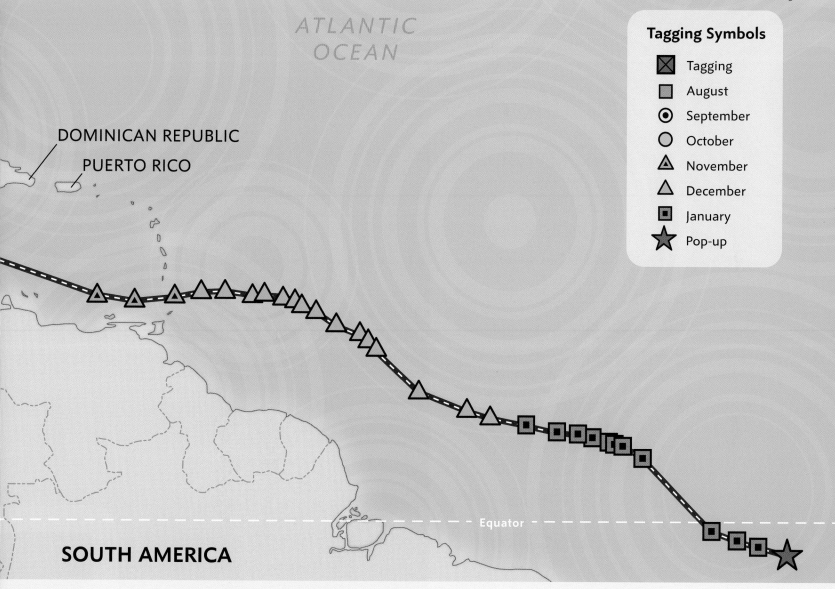

Tracking Rio Lady

Tagging Symbols

⊠ Tagging
◼ August
◉ September
◯ October
△ November
△ December
▣ January
★ Pop-up

ATLANTIC OCEAN

DOMINICAN REPUBLIC

PUERTO RICO

SOUTH AMERICA

Equator

Hueter's team tracked Rio Lady for 150 days and 5,000 miles (8,046 km) before the PSAT fell off. She led them to a part of the ocean halfway between South America and Africa. Rafael de la Parra, who was working with Robert Hueter, said, "We think, maybe, pregnant females are trying to reach the intercontinental ridges to release their pups where the ocean is very deep."

Whale shark researcher Jennifer Schmidt said, "In fact, we only see the adult females who could be pupping in a few places on the planet . . . [such as] mid-Atlantic open-ocean areas," areas where the ocean is especially deep.

This discovery made researchers wonder whether whale shark pups might dive and stay deep during the daytime, while they're small, and only swim up to the surface at night to feed. That would help them avoid big predators, such as great white sharks and orcas, which usually hunt near the surface in daylight. Researchers remain uncertain about this theory, though, because whale sharks usually avoid cold water, and deep water is cold. But Jennifer Schmidt said, "Still, the ocean depths are the only place we haven't yet looked for whale shark pups." One thing was certain: however they managed it, some whale shark pups were surviving, because the ones researchers were spotting were mainly juveniles.

To grow bigger, young whale sharks have to swim to the surface where there is plenty of small prey to eat.

Scientists estimate that fishing boats catch up to six hundred whale sharks every year.

Researchers have had few opportunities to study how quickly young whale sharks grow, other than a few captive juveniles in aquariums. These have grown quickly, so perhaps pups living free in the ocean also grow quickly. Of course, those juveniles in captivity had all they needed to eat without any risk.

What about the two trapped juvenile male whale sharks? Can they escape the fishing net and keep on growing?

RESCUED!

Luckily, help is nearby. Researchers on board a boat from the Global Whale Shark Research Program with the Marine Megafauna Foundation see the fishing boat crew working hard but not pulling in the net. They guess it's because whale sharks are in the net. They motor close, and two divers jump into the water and swim over the top of the net's edge to try to help.

While the divers work to free the whale sharks, the boat's crew finally succeeds in lowering one side of the net. The larger male swims across the floats into open water. A moment later, the smaller whale shark's fin is untangled, and it follows the larger male across the edge of the net.

The diver works to free the whale shark tangled in the net.

To the divers' surprise, one whale shark swims alongside until they reach their boat. Perhaps it's the juvenile's way of saying thank you.

The trapped whale sharks are *free*! On the deck, the members of the research team exchange smiles. This is a happy moment. The survival of two healthy young males offers a little more hope for the future of the whale shark population.

Thanks to the mysteries scientists have solved, people now have a better understanding of whale shark behavior and what they need to live. The key is protecting ocean areas where these giants gather to feed—even as those gathering sites change. It's also important to keep whale sharks safe along the marine pathways they regularly follow, migrating through the oceans. Though the United Nations has set a target of protecting 10 percent of the oceans by 2020, currently less than 3 percent are marine reserves.

More needs to be done quickly to preserve whale shark populations. Whale sharks are key members of their ocean ecosystems. Jennifer Schmidt said, "I think there are essential roles for any species in an ecosystem, and whale sharks certainly have a huge effect where they gather [to feed]."

It could be we won't know how valuable whale sharks are to the balance of life in Earth's oceans unless they're gone.

GREAT WHITE SHARKS NEED HELP TOO

More than four hundred shark species swim the seas, but one of the best known is the great white shark. As of 2017, the IUCN labeled it Vulnerable. Being strong and having a mouthful of three hundred teeth makes the great white shark one of the top ocean predators, but that's not enough to save them. The great white shark population has seriously decreased after years of people fishing for them to collect their fins and their teeth, and to display them as trophies. So researchers are using the same new technologies used to study whale sharks to study great white shark behavior in order to help them.

Researchers have already discovered some great whites have seasonal migrations. So they're studying those migration routes and working to understand what conditions—even what parts of the ocean—great white sharks need to live and reproduce. Then researchers can ask countries to restrict fishing for great whites in those areas. Some protective measures are already in place. For example, a number of countries have laws banning any shark fishing within a set distance of the coast. Many other countries have laws against selling any shark products. Unfortunately, laws aren't enough. People need to fear great whites less and value them more. As top predators, they're key members of the ocean ecosystem they inhabit.

Author's Note

I love digging into a mystery. Learning that so many mysteries still need to be solved about whale sharks caught my attention—especially when I learned this ocean giant had recently been downgraded from Vulnerable to Endangered. I was also eager to jump into the research for this story because it was my chance to learn about ocean expeditions and research into the life and behavior of the biggest shark in the ocean. Of course, I enjoyed talking to experts about their dive experiences. I love snorkeling to explore ocean life myself. Some of my favorite memories are those times I spent immersed in the underwater world, with its liquid feel, different light and shadows, and amazing plants and animals.

My thanks to all the whale shark experts around the world who gave so willingly of their time and shared their innovative whale shark research efforts. I was also impressed with the awe they expressed describing whale sharks. For example, Robert Hueter said, "Being in the water with one, you sense its immense power, and yet it's very graceful."

And Rafael de la Parra called whale sharks "majestic."

I'm grateful for all those making an effort to understand the mysterious lives of whale sharks. After all, understanding them is the only way we'll really know how to help them continue to exist and play their role in ocean ecosystems.

Did You Know?

Remoras (suckerfish) sometimes attach themselves to a whale shark. They feed on the small parasites, particularly copepods (small crustacean cousins of crabs), that cling to its skin. So remoras keep the whale shark's skin clean.

Scientists believe whale sharks live to be seventy to one hundred years old.

Whale sharks, like other sharks, must swim to breathe. Swimming is what pushes water through their gills.

Researchers report that whale sharks are so sensitive to what they take into their mouths while feeding that they'll pause and cough out some things, such as jellyfish.

Timeline

1828   Dr. Andrew Smith discovers a whale shark off the coast of South Africa. He identifies it as the world's largest kind of shark.

1933   Eugene Gudger first notices large numbers of whale sharks gathering for four to five months (with the largest numbers in July and August) off the coast of Mexico's Yucatán Peninsula.

1980   Whale sharks remain largely unstudied with only 320 recorded sightings in the 152 years since their discovery in 1828.

1986   National Geographic marine biologist Greg Marshall invents the Crittercam.

1987   Ningaloo Marine Park is established in Australia.

1995   A commercial fishing boat catches a pregnant female whale shark off Taiwan. An examination reveals more than three hundred pups inside her uterus.

       Brad Norman founds ECOCEAN, with participation by fifty-four countries, to share research and encourage conservation of whale sharks.

1999   The whale shark is listed as Vulnerable and Migratory under Australia's Environment Protection and Biodiversity Conservation Act.

2000   The International Union for Conservation of Nature (ICUN) Red List identifies whale sharks as Vulnerable.

2002   The Convention for International Trade in Endangered Species includes global protection against trade in whale shark products within the 160-member countries. Other sharks have been included since 1994.

2003   Scientists begin monitoring large numbers of whale sharks gathering off the cost of Mexico's Yucatán Peninsula for four to five months—the largest numbers are during July and August.

2005   The Australian government begins a whale shark recovery plan.

2007   A pregnant whale shark nicknamed Rio Lady is tracked using a PSAT to the part of the Atlantic Ocean between Brazil and Africa.

2009   The Mexican government establishes Reserva de la Biosfera Tiburón Ballena (the Whale Shark Biosphere Reserve) next to the existing natural reserve of Yum Balam. The largest gathering of whale sharks ever reported to date is discovered in an area called the *afuera* outside the Biosfera Tiburón Ballena. A single aerial survey of 11 miles (18 km) of ocean showed 420 whale sharks.

2010 The United States passes the Shark Conservation Act to restrict high-seas commercial fishing and improve conservation of all types of sharks.

2013 Liquid Robotics announces a breakthrough in ocean observation with the introduction of Wave Glider SV3.

2015 Researchers first successfully attach a fin-mounted SAT to track whale sharks. The Whale Shark and Oceanic Research Center teams up with Liquid Robotics to begin a project using drones to track whale sharks with acoustic tags.

2016 The whale shark status on the International Union for Conservation of Nature Red List changes from Vulnerable to Endangered.

Ecuador creates a marine reserve around Galápagos Islands as large as the country of Belgium, because of the area's noted high number of sharks.

Mexico creates three new marine reserves: the Pacific Islands Biosphere Reserve, the Pacific Islands Biosphere Reserve, and the Mexican Caribbean Biosphere Reserve.

Source Notes

9   James Sulikowski, telephone interview with the author, November 12, 2018.

19   Simon Pierce, telephone interview with the author, July 17, 2017.

21   Rafael de la Parra, telephone interview with the author, July 11, 2017.

24   Pierce, interview.

33   De la Parra, interview.

34   Jennifer Schmidt, telephone interview with the author, August 22, 2017.

34   Schmidt.

38   Schmidt.

42   Robert Hueter, telephone interview with the author, August 1, 2017.

42   De la Parra, interview.

Glossary

clasper: a part of a pelvic fin found on an adult male shark

dorsal fin: the tall, triangular fin that's on the top of a shark's back

ecosystem: living things and the physical environment in which they live

ecotourism: traveling to threatened environments to support conservation efforts and observe wildlife

endangered: species populations that are in severe decline and are at risk for extinctions based on several factors, such as pollution, deforestation, and hunting

gill: the body part in fish that lets it breathe by taking oxygen from the water

juvenile: the young whale shark stage between pup and mature adult

migration: the movement of animals from one area to another

pectoral fin: a fin on either side of a fish, just behind the fish's head, which helps the fish steer

pelvic fin: a fin on either side of a fish's abdomen, which helps it steer

phytoplankton: tiny plants that form the base of the ocean food chain

pup: a baby whale shark

species: a kind of living thing

upwelling: when surface winds push warm surface water away from the shore and deeper, colder water rises up to replace it, bringing nutrients up with it

uterus: a body part inside the female shark's belly where pups develop

vulnerable: a species facing threats, such as loss of habitat and poaching, in the wild that may cause it to go extinct

zooplankton: tiny marine animals plus immature stages of larger animals

Find Out More

Check out these books and websites to discover even more:

Cerullo, Mary. *Seeking Giant Sharks: A Shark Diver's Quest for Whale Sharks, Basking Sharks, and Manta Rays*. North Mankato, MN: Compass Point Books, 2014.
Follow noted diving photographer Jeff Rotman into the ocean to share his firsthand experiences with whale sharks and their giant cousins.

DK. *Super Shark Encyclopedia: And Other Creatures of the Deep*. New York: DK Children's Publishing, 2015.
Compare whale sharks to other kinds of sharks. How are they similar? How are they different?

Whale Shark Fact File
http://www.arkive.org/whale-shark/rhincodon-typus/video-01b.html
Watch these short videos to dive underwater and get up close to whale sharks.

Whale Shark Night Feeding! A Video by Craig Capehart
https://www.youtube.com/watch?v=lpbNjGk2r98&feature=youtu.be
This rare footage shows a group of whale sharks feeding at night, pulling water and fish in to their huge mouths. You can see—and hear—the suction force they create as they feed.

Whale Shark Research Project
http://whalesharkrp.com
Follow different whale shark research projects and discover amazing facts about whale sharks.

Wildbook for Whale Sharks
https://www.whaleshark.org
Check out the ever-changing current number of identified whale sharks.

Williams, Lily. *If Sharks Disappeared*. New York: Roaring Brook, 2017.
A girl in a boat acts as a guide to show readers what could happen to ocean ecosystems if sharks became extinct.

Index

birth, 31
breathing, 10–11, 43

climate change, 14, 16, 20
commercial fishing, 13–14, 20, 31, 35–36, 41
Crittercam, 28

de la Parra, Rafael, 21, 33, 42

ecotourism, 20

food, 4, 10, 14–15, 17–19, 26, 28, 31, 34, 38

gathering sites, 14–17, 20–21, 32, 38
Global Whale Shark Research Program, 36
Goldilocks factor, 16, 27

Hueter, Robert, 32–33, 42

identification, 8–9, 29
International Union for Conservation of Nature, 9, 41

juveniles, 4, 7, 9, 13, 24, 34–35, 37

maps, 16, 20, 24–25, 32–33
migration, 16–17, 24, 27, 38, 41

Norman, Brad, 29

ocean reserves, 20–21

phytoplankton, 14, 19, 26
Pierce, Simon, 19, 24, 29
population, 8–9, 15, 24, 37–38, 41

pop-up satellite archival tag (PSAT), 24–25, 33
pups, 24, 30–35
purse seine net, 6–7

satellite archival tag (SAT), 22–24
Schmidt, Jennifer, 34, 38
shipping lanes, 17
Sulikowski, James, 9

upwelling, 14, 20

Wave Glider SV3, 26–27
whales, 10
Wildbook for Whale Sharks, 8, 29

zooplankton, 14–15, 18, 26

Photo Acknowledgments

Image credits: Jones/Shimlock-Secret Sea Visions/Getty Images, p. 1; Borut Furlan/Getty Images, pp. 4, 5; © Simon Pierce, pp. 6, 9, 29, 36, 37; Laura Westlund/Independent Picture Service, pp. 7, 14, 16, 20, 23, 24–25, 32–33; wildestanimal/Getty Images, pp. 8, 9, 35; Auscape/UIG/Getty Images, p. 9; seanscott/Getty Images, p. 10; Steve De Neef/VW Pics/UIG/Getty Images, p. 11; ASIF HASSAN/AFP/Getty Images, p. 12; Luis Javier Sandoval/VW Pics/UIG/Getty Images, p. 15; © Mauricio Handler/National Geographic Stock, pp. 17, 43; © Jurgen Freund/naturepl.com, p. 18; wildestanimal/Getty Images, p. 19; Jurgen Freund/Nature Picture Library/Getty Images, p. 22; © Jeff Rotman/Minden Pictures, p. 26; © Mark Thiessen/National Geographic Stock, p. 28; © Lilia González, p. 29; Courtesy of Liquid Robotics, p. 29; Jason Holmberg/Wildbook for Whale Sharks, p. 29; © Andre Seale/SeaPics.com, pp. 30, 31; Rodrigo Friscione/Getty Images, p. 34; James D. Morgan/Getty Images, p. 38, 39; © David B. Fleetham/SeaPics.com, p. 40; ullstein bild/Getty Images, p. 42.

Cover Image: Andrey Nekrasov/Alamy Stock Photo.

Design Elements: Airin.dizain/Shutterstock.com.